Original title:
The Great Life Experiment: Still Ongoing

Copyright © 2025 Creative Arts Management OÜ
All rights reserved.

Author: Samuel Kensington
ISBN HARDBACK: 978-1-80566-278-5
ISBN PAPERBACK: 978-1-80566-573-1

Time's Relentless Canvas

Tick-tock goes the clock, paint spills everywhere,
Blank canvas of my days, laughter fills the air.
Brush strokes of mishaps, colorful and bright,
Each smear a reminder of my daily plight.

Coffee spills at dawn, a masterpiece in brown,
Pants too tight, a canvas wrapping round.
Life's a funny painting, splattered, yet divine,
In a gallery of chaos, I call it all mine.

Balancing Acts of the Heart

Juggling love and laundry, oh what a sight!
Fell in love with a sock, now it's taking flight.
Twirling on the line, bright colors in a spin,
My heart's a circus, let the show begin!

Hoping for romance while chasing down my cat,
Every date's a tightrope, where I might fall flat.
Yet I laugh at the tumble, the mess I create,
For love's a big adventure, no time to wait!

Waves of Curiosity Lapping At The Shore

Curiosity knocks, a wave crashes near,
Thinking of embracing each splashing cheer.
Seashells whisper secrets, tides pull me around,
In the ocean of wonder, joy can be found.

Dipping toes in thought, shall I dive today?
The sea of the unknown, where fish fear to play.
With laughter as my buoy, I float on bright dreams,
Each wave of discovery bursts forth with beams.

A Journey Beyond the Horizon

On the road to nowhere, my map's upside down,
Every turn is a giggle, no reason to frown.
Lost at every junction, but joy is the guide,
For every wrong turn, there's peace at my side.

Chasing sunsets goofy, shoes two sizes too big,
Dance like no one's watching, do a moonwalk jig.
The horizon is winking, with mischief in store,
Let's stumble through life, who could ask for more?

Threads of Destiny Weaving Together

In the fabric of mishaps and dreams,
We stitch together life's wildest schemes.
A sock on the roof, a hat on the cat,
We laugh as we wonder, 'What's up with that?'

Colors collide in the most wacky ways,
A dance of the socks in a rainbow haze.
With threads of confusion, we knot and pull tight,
Creating a tapestry that's just out of sight.

In the Midst of Becoming

Juggling careers like balloons in the air,
One's lost to a cactus, another to hair.
With each awkward moment, we learn how to sway,
Embracing the goofy that brightens our day.

Building our futures on laughter and fate,
We trip over troubles, but still find the great.
In the midst of our journeys, we stumble and glide,
A dance of the clueless, with joy as our guide.

After the Storms Pass

When clouds turn to cotton candy fluff,
And puddles reflect all things silly and tough.
We march through the rain with our mismatched shoes,
Creating a splash with every odd move.

The rainbow appears, wearing sparkly shoes,
As rainbows are known for their colorful views.
With umbrellas like hats, we laugh and we cheer,
For the laughter we share is what makes things clear.

Harmonies of Hope and Hesitation

In the melody of hiccups, we find our refrain,
Each note is a blunder, a smile, and a gain.
With whispers of doubts wrapped in giggles so bright,
We create an encore that feels just right.

Swaying to rhythms that twist and that bend,
We sing to the future with laughter as our friend.
In the chorus of life, we may fumble and fall,
But together, we rise—it's the best part of all.

Embracing the Beautiful Unknown

Jump into the void with flair,
Wear mismatched socks, show you care.
Tickle the stars, chase the moonlight,
Dance with shadows, it feels just right.

Slip on banana peels with glee,
Laugh at the chaos, let it be free.
Chase wild dreams, don't be a bore,
Life's a circus, come see the show floor!

The Alchemy of Living Boldly

Mix a potion of laughter and cheer,
Sprinkle in some joy, hold it dear.
Whisk in a dash of daring delight,
Sauté your fears, make them take flight.

Cook up some laughs, serve them hot,
Take a leap, give it a shot.
Life's a recipe, oh so sprightly,
Let's bake a cake — not too rightly!

Reflections in a Kaleidoscope

Flip through the colors, they swirl and spin,
Catch a glimpse of the silly within.
Shiny distractions, oh what a show,
Lost and found in a whimsy flow.

Mirror, mirror, who's the goof?
A riddle wrapped in a dance of poof!
Giggles echo, a tune so grand,
Join the parade, lend a hand!

A Canvas of Unfinished Stories

Brush the canvas with imagination,
Splatter paint like a wild celebration.
Sketch out dreams on a whimsy train,
Splash of joy, a sprinkle of rain.

Hang the oddities, let them gleam,
Draft a tale, burst at the seam.
Life's a gallery, full of the bizarre,
Every moment, a wild memoir!

Adventures in the Realm of What-Ifs

What if cats ruled the land?
Would I still wear socks so grand?
Chasing mice with laser beams,
Daydreaming of candy streams.

What if fish could ride a bike?
Paddling past on a strike
While birds offer witty quips,
And squirrels do acrobat flips?

What if trees became our mates?
Hoisting teas on wooden plates?
Gossiping with summer bees,
Underneath the rustling leaves.

What if clouds played hide and seek?
Switching shades from bold to meek?
I'd wave at them from below,
And join in this cosmic show.

The Dance of Serendipity

Dancing shoes on Sunday morn,
I twirl and trip on twisty corn.
A balloon floats by my head,
And giggles fill the room instead.

Unplanned trips to the local park,
Where squirrels steal my crumbs, oh hark!
They dance a jig, a cheeky thing,
As I muse on the joy they bring.

Fortune cookies laughing loud,
Predictions made, I feel so proud.
But all they say is 'Try again,'
As I munch down my chocolate then.

In the rhythm of the strange and new,
Each moment counts, this much is true.
With serendipity in twirling bliss,
I laugh at life's chaotic twist!

Unleashing the Winds of Change

The wind whispered secrets in my ear,
Said, 'Let's run wild, let's have no fear!'
I donned my cape made of old sheets,
And zoomed past cows with funny tweets.

Baking muffins that fly off the rack,
They bounce around, "Don't hold me back!"
The dog joins in, a tail of glee,
As crumbs become a feast for thee.

What if socks had their own parade?
Dancing about, truly unafraid?
While flip-flops sing their silly songs,
In a world where everything belongs.

Change is just a breeze away,
With laughter brightening the day.
Let's unleash the wild and free,
Embrace the chaos, you and me!

The Art of Falling and Rising

Oh, the art of tripping on my shoes,
And laughing with joy about my blues.
Gravity's grip, so stubborn and tight,
But I leap like a deer in the midst of night.

Falling flat with pie on my face,
Curious looks, and outer space.
A dance to the ground, a grandiose fall,
But I spring up quick; I'm having a ball!

With each tumble, I ponder the art,
Of rolling along with a froggy heart.
Why not bounce like a rubber ball,
Embracing the fate of the great and small?

So step lightly, with laughter in tow,
For life's a circus, in this grand show.
We fall, we rise, it's all such a breeze,
As we dance through life with ultimate ease!

Fragments of a Wandering Soul

I lost my keys in a loaf of bread,
Thought they were gone, but they were just spread.
Chasing shadows of my laundry pile,
Each sock a ghost, haunting my style.

Eating cake for dinner feels quite divine,
Dessert first, that's my master design.
With a map made of crumbs and strange memes,
I wander through life on a pathway of dreams.

Seasons of Uncertain Growth

Spring brings blossoms and sneezing fits,
While summer's sun gives me scorching hits.
Autumn leaves dance in a flurry of fun,
And winter's chill whispers, 'Where's everyone?'

I tried planting hopes in a garden of fears,
But they sprouted doubts through the laughter and tears.
Each season changes; the weather, a trick,
Like my plans for dinner – I just can't pick!

Paths Yet to Be Walked

I took a stroll down the road less traveled,
But my feet got stuck where the puzzles unraveled.
Each turn I made led to ice cream stands,
With sprinkles and laughter spilling from hands.

The map said 'Go', but I think it was wrong,
Lead me to karaoke, where I don't belong.
With each note I croak, the crowd shuffles away,
Yet I'm still dancing like it's the highlight of my day.

The Dance of Days Unspent

Life's a jig, done in mismatched shoes,
Twisting and turning, sipping on blues.
With friends in a whirl, we gather our hopes,
Each twirl a chance to laugh, and elope.

Waking up late, 'cause who needs the sun?
We rise with the moon; isn't that fun?
Dreams turn to stardust, we catch in delight,
As the dance floor spins, we glide into night.

Journey Through Unwritten Pages

We scribble notes on napkins dear,
While coffee spills remind us here.
The plot thickens with every cup,
As characters jump and hiccup up.

We chase our dreams on paper boats,
With rubber ducks and silly quotes.
Each twist and turn, a chuckle loud,
As we trip on dreams beneath a cloud.

In doodled sketches, we draw our fate,
With crayons bright, we contemplate.
A paper chase through twists and bends,
Making laughter from the trends.

So let's embrace the wild unknown,
In every misstep, laughter's grown.
With pages blank, we make our mark,
Chasing magic in the dark.

Chronicles of Uncertainty's Dance

In a world where plans go askew,
We dance with doubts in our best shoe.
With two left feet, we take a chance,
And twirl through chaos in a trance.

Each step a giggle, every twirl,
As life spins on, we laugh and swirl.
The future calls, but we just prance,
In ill-fitting suits, we make our stance.

With pie charts made of whipped cream pies,
We analyze until we realize:
The answers hide in silly moments,
As we craft joy in funny components.

So here's to wobbles in our fate,
To jigs and jives that make us wait.
We'll giggle loud as we misstep,
In this wild dance, we'll take a rep.

Threads of Tomorrow's Tapestry

We weave our dreams with bits of string,
With every knot, we laugh and sing.
Embroidery of hopes and fears,
We stitch them all with happy tears.

The fabric frays, yet still we sew,
Creating patterns from what we know.
In tangled threads, we find the art,
Of making whole from every part.

With mismatched socks and colors bright,
Our vision's bold, a playful sight.
Each thread a tale, each patch a cheer,
We quilt our futures, year by year.

So grab your needle, let's create,
A tapestry that celebrates.
In every loop, we'll find delight,
In the messiness of our flight.

Moments Caught in Time's Embrace

We freeze our laughs in jars so neat,
With memories sweet, a tasty treat.
Each giggle captured, every smile,
In snapshots paused, we savor style.

Like jelly beans in colors bright,
Our moments burst with pure delight.
A belly flop or silly face,
We savor life at its own pace.

The clock may tick, the hourglass wane,
Yet in our hearts, we'll dance in rain.
With every tick, we make a scene,
A playful peek, a look unseen.

So here's to time that loves to play,
To silly moments brightening our day.
We'll spin and twirl in memories' race,
In the joyful chaos of our space.

The Palette of Experience

In a splash of color, we dive right in,
With brushes of laughter, let the oddness begin.
Cerulean moods mix with shades of surprise,
As our canvas unfolds with no need for disguise.

The reds of our failures, the yellows of cheer,
A portrait of mishaps that we hold so dear.
Dancing with joy in this crazy ballet,
Each stroke tells a story, in its own quirky way.

Navigating the Unmapped

With a map that's all scribbles and some coffee spillage,
We wander through life, following each silly village.
GPS says 'recalculating,' but we just giggle,
On pathways obscure, as our minds take a wiggle.

Each twist and turn is a plot that unfolds,
Finding treasures in moments, more precious than gold.
So here's to the detours, the scenic and hazy,
In the journey of laughter, it's never too crazy.

Footprints of Potential Lost and Found

We leave trails of giggles upon shifting sands,
Tracking dreams that escape like quick, slippery hands.
In the chaos of choices, we sometimes trip down,
But we dust off our egos and wear silly crowns.

With footprints so quirky, each tells its tale,
Of misunderstandings and epic fail.
Yet in every misstep, we find something grand,
The dance of our lives, perfectly unplanned.

Stories Yet to Be Told

In the book of our lives, the pages are blank,
With scribbles of laughter and a wink that we crank.
Characters waiting, with quirks to unfold,
A plot line that twists, worth its weight in gold.

Like socks without partners, they wait in the drawer,
For adventures that beckon and open the door.
So grab your best quill and let's make a scene,
In this comic book life, where we reign as the queen!

Tentative Steps on a Dreamer's Journey

With feet so light, I tiptoe through,
A world that whispers, "Try something new!"
I trip on hopes like scattered leaves,
And laugh at what my foolish heart believes.

The map is drawn in crayon lines,
I navigate through tangled vines.
Each twist and turn, a comical dance,
Fumbling dreams, but I still take a chance.

With sleep in my eyes, I greet the sun,
And wonder how each day could be fun.
The coffee's strong, but my wit is stronger,
In this quirky race, I just can't linger.

As laughter spills like marbles on floors,
I gather them up, each joke I explores.
Though wobbly steps may lead to a fall,
I'll always get up, laughing through it all.

Unseen Corners of Possibility

A sock without a partner, it makes me grin,
Perhaps it dances with a cat or a tin.
In every drawer, adventures hide,
Where lost ideas and snacks reside.

Under the bed, dust bunnies leap,
Who knew they held secrets so far from sleep?
They giggle as I stumble and frown,
In these corners, my dreams wear a crown.

I peek under cushions, find coins of fate,
In silly pursuits, I sometimes wait.
With laughter echoing off the walls,
I make a fort that magically calls.

So here's to the paths less traveled near,
Where possibilities bloom and dance with cheer.
With humor sprouting like daisies in spring,
I embrace the strange wonders these corners bring.

Flickers of Joy in Uncertain Times

In a world that spins like a topsy tale,
I chase after giggles, can't let them fail.
With each silly stumble, my spirits rise,
As joy flickers like stars in cloudy skies.

There's a dance in my heart with mismatched shoes,
And a chorus of chuckles wherever I choose.
When plans go awry, I find the delight,
Like finding a flashlight in the middle of night.

Of course, there's worry; it knocks on my door,
But I shoo it away with a wink and a roar.
The frosting's too sweet, the cake's a bit odd,
Yet it's these little moments I'm thankful to laud.

So here's to the days when nothing feels right,
When laughter's the compass, our hearts take flight.
Through ups and downs, a whimsical maze,
These flickers of joy light up all our days.

Breathless Moments of Awakening

Awake! The rooster crows, and I'm still in bed,
Chasing the dreams that danced in my head.
With a yawn that could rattle the stars,
I grab my coffee and laugh at my scars.

There are moments that leave me gasping for air,
Like when I trip over thoughts that don't care.
As butterflies tickle my fancy anew,
I find myself giggling at skies so blue.

Lightning bugs blink like they've missed the cue,
And I'm there with a net, trying to catch a few.
In the chaos of life, I'm breathless, it's true,
Yet laughter wraps 'round like the soft morning dew.

So breathe in the odd, embrace every jest,
In this wild waking, I'm simply the best.
With each joyful moment, my spirit takes flight,
Dancing through life, from morning to night.

Heartbeats of the Unexplored

In the maze of quirky paths,
Where squirrels wear hats and dance,
We trip on our own two feet,
Laughing at every chance.

The sun shines in the wrong direction,
While clouds plot shy and tease,
We follow the whims of fate,
Like fish that climb up trees.

Every turn brings a surprise,
A pie on my head, oh my!
With every bump and tumble,
I don't know whether to cry.

Yet through the giggles and slips,
Adventure is surely near,
With each beat of our wild hearts,
We shed a joyful tear.

The Rhythm of Unpredictable Turns

Like a yo-yo in the wind,
Life spins us 'round and 'round,
We waltz with chaos daily,
To a tune that's quite profound.

The calendar plays tricks on me,
As Mondays don't seem so sweet,
I'm juggling flaming cupcakes now,
While dancing on my feet.

Every time I think I'm set,
A plot twist pulls my sleeve,
With cupcakes pulling pranks, I'll bet,
Who would dare to believe?

Yet amidst this merry mess,
There's laughter to be found,
In every tumble, jolt, and guess,
Life's rhythm is quite sound.

Secrets Woven in Shadow and Dawn

In the twilight of our secrets,
We chuckle with glee at night,
The moon winks at hidden truths,
As day gives way to light.

Ghosts of plans once neatly laid,
Dance like pixies under the stars,
Who knew socks could talk, I swear,
And offer advice from Mars?

With every shadow that we chase,
A riddle wrapped in fun,
Why did the chicken cross the road?
Oh, just to see the sun.

So here's to the whispers we keep,
Crafted under moonbeams bright,
Every secret shared with laughter,
Makes wandering so right.

Mosaics of Hope and Doubt

In a room filled with odd socks,
A puzzle where pieces don't fit,
We gather our hopes like coins,
    Each one a quirky bit.

The recipes come with a twist,
Like pickles in my sweet pie,
With every spoonful of laughter,
    I wonder how and why.

Doubt dances with a playful grin,
As we mix mischief and fun,
Will this color match that shade?
Let's paint with a runaway sun!

Yet through the mosaic we create,
Each piece shines with delight,
For in the strange mix of all,
We craft the dreams of night.

Seeds of Change in a Shifting World

In a garden so wild, it's a bramble of glee,
Planting jokes with the seeds that we see.
Sunflowers dancing, the weeds tell a tale,
Of laughter and chaos, and stories that prevail.

The carrots wear glasses, they think they're quite smart,
While radishes giggle, they play the best part.
Dandelions frolic, spreading puffball dreams,
In a world that keeps changing, nothing's as it seems.

Interludes of Hesitation

A pause at the crossroads, a squirrel thinks it through,
Should I go left for the acorns or right for the view?
The traffic light flashes, but the turtle thinks slow,
He'll cross when he's ready, just taking it low.

A cat on the fence shakes its head at the scene,
It's a fine day for napping, if you know what I mean.
People all rushing, they trip on their feet,
While dogs by the lamppost save energy to greet.

Points of Light in the Shadowlands

In shadows they flicker, like fireflies at dusk,
Finding joy in the darkness, in crevices of trust.
A moth with a mission, chasing each glow,
Turned disco ball lights in a play of tableau.

They dance on expectations, with chuckles and cheer,
Finding humor in quirks that the day may hold dear.
A lantern's bright laughter, a beacon that shines,
Turning gloom into giggles with whimsical lines.

Kaleidoscope of Life's Questions

Turn the dial on your thoughts, what colors appear?
Are we all just a puzzle with pieces unclear?
Questions like marbles, rolling all around,
In the game of existence, where fun can be found.

Why did the chicken cross paths bright and bold?
Perhaps it was searching for stories untold.
With each little twist, new visions unfurl,
In this wacky adventure, let's laugh and twirl.

Diverging Trails of Tomorrow's Paths

Two paths diverged; one led to snacks,
The other promised wisdom and hacks.
I chose the snacks, with a twisty grin,
Now I'm wise, but only about din!

In a world where choices all collide,
I pick the wild ones, let chaos decide.
With every step, I trip on fate,
And laugh as the future can't wait!

Maps are for those who like to plan,
I'm more of a wanderer, a risqué fan.
Each turn I take, a new plot thickens,
Surprises await, with laughter that sickens.

So raise a toast to the awkward dance,
Where fortune smiles at the barest chance.
We'll stumble through moments, quick-witted and spry,
In this wild maze, oh my, oh my!

Epiphany Beneath the Stardust

Under the stars with my sandwich in hand,
I ponder deep questions that twist and expand.
Did I leave the oven on? Oh, what a thrill!
Maybe that's stardust, or just my own grill!

An epiphany strikes with a cosmic fright,
As I muse on my dreams and the universe's plight.
Is life just a game, and am I behind?
I'll catch up next round, just give me some wine!

With every shooting star, my hopes take flight,
Each culinary mishap squares up for a bite.
Should I grill veggies or make a pie crust?
Well, let's be real, it may crumble to dust!

So here's to the moments we can't comprehend,
To the stars, the snacks, and the friends that we tend.
Life's a buffet of chaotic delight,
And I'm loaded with laughter, not fear of the night!

Embers of a Thousand Possibilities

In the hearth's glow, the embers ignite,
A flicker of dreams to become my delight.
I try to roast marshmallows, but they end up charred,
A smoky reminder that life's not too hard.

Every spark's a path, a dance to explore,
Yet half of my journeys end up at the door.
I set out to conquer, but often I roam,
With marshmallows stuck to my shirt as my home.

Potentials abound like stars in the night,
But I'm still wrestling with oven light.
"Cook something great!" echo my hopes through the air,
But somehow, it's just burnt edges and flair!

So let the embers crackle, as chaos blooms,
In laughter and trials, we shatter our glooms.
For whether I bake or I simply combust,
It's the fun of it all that earns my trust!

Chance Encounters with Destiny's Brush

On this path of chance, I stumbled a bit,
Met destiny's brush—ain't life just a skit?
I tripped over fate with a comic finesse,
And gained a new hairstyle, oh what a mess!

Painting the days with colors uncouth,
Every slip of the brush leads to comic truth.
I doodle my dreams on the backs of my hands,
With ink that just smudges—and yet, life still stands.

With each twist of fate, there's laughter, not frowns,
My dance with destiny wears odd little crowns.
In the gallery of life, each slip is a prize,
So I grin as the universe rolls its eyes.

So here's to those brushes that boldly collide,
With colors so wild, it's a crazy ride!
Are we art? Or just messy expressions of cheer?
In this wild masterpiece, I've nothing to fear!

Lighthouses of Hope Across the Sea

Oh, the boats that bob and weave,
With seagulls scheming overhead.
They squawk and cackle, never leave,
While fish just can't be bothered, fed.

The lighthouse beams shine through the fog,
A beacon bright for wayward folk.
But here I sit, a sloth-like slog,
And contemplate my swim for smoke.

The crabs are dancing on the shore,
Their pinching game's a sight to see.
Yet here I am, not wanting more,
Just sipping my cold iced tea.

With every wave, I wonder why
The jellyfish decide to float.
They wave their tentacles, oh my!
I'd rather take a ferry boat.

Meditations on What Lies Ahead

I ponder life like a sock on sale,
Lost in piles of mismatched wear.
What's the point of all this gale?
Is fortune found with dirty hair?

Each morning's coffee brings a dream,
Of dancing ducks in feathered coats.
They waddle, quack, and form a team,
While I just hope, avoid the oats.

The future's bright as a traffic light,
Yet sometimes green just means to pause.
I'll take a stroll, a chance to fight,
For every laugh, I'll find a cause.

So here's to flops and ticking clocks,
To every slip and every trip.
Life's a parade of polka-dots,
Let's raise a cheer, and not a sip!

Life's Unscripted Symphony

In a world where plans go awry,
The chicken dances, oh my, oh my!
I juggle dreams like a clown in a tent,
Each twist and turn, a giggle well spent.

The coffee spills like a rushing stream,
I sip it slow, still chase that dream.
With every note, the trumpet honks loud,
Life's melody makes us all feel proud.

A cat on the piano, what a sight!
Playing chords that don't feel quite right.
Yet in this chaos, joy can be found,
As laughter echoes, profound and unbound.

So here's to the rhythm, messy and grand,
To all the dancers with no master plan.
Let the symphony play, let it roar,
In this funny ballet, who could ask for more?

Reflections on a Flickering Flame

A candle winks, a flame that prances,
Dancing shadows, wild romances.
Each flicker whispers tales untold,
Of socks unmatched and bread that's mold.

In my kitchen, the smoke alarms sing,
While I attempt culinary bling.
The toast pops up like it's had a fright,
A breakfast show gone wrong, what a sight!

The flame remembers all my misdeeds,
Like burning cookies and odd-shaped reeds.
Yet through the chaos, laughter ignites,
A symphony of fun through playful nights.

So let it flicker, let it gleam bright,
Our life's a show with twists and delight.
With every candle that happens to burn,
We celebrate lessons, oh what a turn!

Mosaic of Expectations and Realities

I envision grandeur, oh such a sight,
But reality has plans that feel contrite.
My dreams, like puzzles, gather some dust,
While socks dance together, in dreams we trust.

A glamorous dinner turns into a feast,
Of takeout boxes that satisfy least.
Each longing slice, a hope dashed away,
As I dine with leftovers, night turns to day.

The grass looks greener on Instagram's shore,
But in my backyard, weeds start to roar.
Yet laughter blooms where chaos has bled,
A whimsical garden, though slightly misled.

So here's to the mess, the joy that we find,
In each quirky twist that life has designed.
Our mosaic shines, every piece a tale,
In this funky adventure, we'll never derail!

The Uncharted Path Ahead

With maps in hand and snacks in tow,
We wander roads we do not know.
Each twist and turn leads us astray,
But oh, the sights we see on the way!

Is that a mountain or a giant mound?
I trip on my shoelace, tumble around.
Yet laughter carries me through the fall,
As squirrels cheer on, giving their all.

We've learned to dance on uneven ground,
With every misstep, we're gloriously crowned.
Our GPS is valid only in jest,
But fortune favors the brave, and we're blessed!

So onward we march, the path unclear,
With a quirky grin and a heart full of cheer.
In this adventure, come what may,
We'll find our way, and laugh all day!

Beneath the Stars of Infinite Questions

Under starlit skies we ponder,
Why do socks vanish? It's a wonder!
Is the universe just one big joke?
Or did aliens steal our last Coke?

With telescopes and laughter loud,
We search the cosmos, oh so proud.
Each twinkle holds a riddle vast,
Did the answer fly by too fast?

As comets race with silly grins,
We chase the truths that life begins.
Will gravity ever take a break?
Or do we float to bake a cake?

So, here we sit with dreams so bright,
Charting stars in the soft moonlight.
The cosmos giggles, a cosmic jest,
For life's sheer chaos is truly blessed.

In Search of the Untold

Seeking secrets in the mundane,
A squirrel's dance makes us feel insane.
What's in that coffee that we sip?
Maybe it's magic, or just a blip.

Each day's a page, a quirky phrase,
In search of laughter through the haze.
Is the mailman really a spy?
Or just a guy who waves goodbye?

Bizarre encounters keep us awake,
Did that cat just learn to break?
Whispers float on the winds of chance,
Life's a wild, unpredictable dance.

Oh, the tales that we could share!
Like when the dog stole Grandpa's chair.
In every laugh, a story waits,
Unveiling laughter that never abates.

Breaths Between the Lines

In life's big book, we flip and scroll,
Finding the humor fills the soul.
Between the lines, we giggle and muse,
Why do we trip in silly shoes?

Late night snacks become our lore,
Who knew chips could spark such lore?
With each crunch, we ponder fate,
As crumbs tumble, we contemplate.

Every awkward pause, a chance to cheer,
Is that a joke we hold so dear?
Between each sentiment, laughter rings,
Life's a symphony of funny things.

So here's to moments we can't quite find,
Like misplaced keys, they tease the mind.
In breaths of laughter, we intertwine,
Creating stories divine over time.

Chasing Fireflies in Dusk's Glow

As day dips low, we run and squeal,
Chasing glimmers, oh what a deal!
Every flicker's a fleeting laugh,
In twilight's game, a playful path.

Fireflies dance like they own the night,
Fleeting sparks in sheer delight.
With each giggle, we trip and fall,
Laughter echoes, it calls us all.

In the glow, we spin and twirl,
Imagining dreams in a shimmering whirl.
What are the odds we'll catch a flight?
With every glow, a new delight!

So let us roam where the small lights dart,
Each moment sparking joy in the heart.
For in the chase, we truly see,
Life is a dance, wild and free.

Unraveled Threads of Existence

In a world made of spaghetti, we twirl,
Life's sauce splatters with every whirl.
Noodles of fate twist and bend,
Laughing, we trip, but never descend.

Pasta or penne, who really knows?
Juggling dreams like tomatoes that froze.
With forks as our compass, we explore,
Finding the flavor amidst chaos galore.

The al dente moments, a perfect bite,
Twirling through kitchen adventures at night.
Sauce stains our shirts, but what do we care?
In this silly dance, joy's everywhere!

So here's to the mess, the laughter we share,
In a pot of perplexity, we throw in a dare.
Life's just funny, a noodle's delight,
With each slurp we savor, everything feels right.

Dreams on the Edge of Discovery

Tiptoeing on clouds made of marshmallow,
Sipping on rain, riding dreams like a cello.
Fingers of sunlight tickle my nose,
In this circus of whimsy, anything goes.

Crispy ideas pop like popcorn kernels,
Floating in thoughts, where reality swirls.
A mind full of giggles, a heart full of zest,
Daring to leap from this infinite nest.

With a trampoline of hope, I bounce and I spin,
The world's a giant playground, let the fun begin!
Chasing the laughter like a runaway kite,
Dreams at the edge, everything feels right.

On this tightrope of wonder, I dance with a grin,
Falling's just winning at life's silly spin.
So here's to the flight, the joy we can share,
In dreams on the edge, there's magic in the air!

The Symphony of Choices Made

In the orchestra of life, I play my flute,
Squeaking out notes, making everything cute.
With decisions like jazz, it's a wild spree,
Twirling through rhythms, just you wait and see.

Choosing between pizza or a slice of cake,
Following whims like a duck on a lake.
With each silly choice, a new twist awaits,
Improv on the stage, no need for debates.

Symphony echoes, a cacophony loud,
With laughter as melody, I spark a crowd.
Each note is a giggle, a playful delight,
In this chaotic concert, everything feels bright.

So don't be too serious, let nonsense unfold,
Life's greatest compositions are often retold.
In the waltz of existence, let laughter parade,
In the symphony's chaos, joy is conveyed.

In Search of Meaning's Light

With a flashlight in hand, I wander the night,
Searching for meaning, but it's just out of sight.
Chasing reflections in puddles of fear,
Every step forward is a giggle, my dear.

Do I look for answers in fruit loops with milk?
Or sip on the stars wrapped in cosmic silk?
Life's puzzles are funny, a riddle unbound,
In this game of existence, new wonders are found.

So I pluck at the strings of tomorrow's tune,
Dancing with shadows beneath the bright moon.
Fumbling with thoughts like an old pair of shoes,
In the quest for the light, I'm just having a snooze.

With humor as compass, I stumble and laugh,
In this journey of life, every slip's a new path.
Here's to the search, the giggles ignite,
In the quest for the meaning, let's revel tonight!

Whispers of the Untraveled Path

In sandals made of squirrel fur,
I wander paths that twist and blur.
The map is useless, lost in thought,
Yet still I stumble, mighty fraught.

With every step, my shoelace breaks,
Dancing like a fish on lakes.
I trip on dreams and trip on fate,
Embracing life and staying late.

A bug just landed on my nose,
I laugh and watch as nature shows.
It seems this journey's quite the ride,
When curiosity's my guide.

So let's toast with cups of cheer,
To all the places yet unclear.
With each misstep, a chance to see,
What wacky wonders will there be?

Dreams on the Edge of Discovery

I tried to leap while wearing boots,
But ended up in garden roots.
The daisies laughed, the sun stood bright,
As I contorted in delight.

Pineapple hats and quirky charms,
Bring all the neighbors to my farms.
A dance-off in a crowded street,
With cows and sheep, we won't retreat.

Jetpacks made of toaster parts,
Are funny dreams that touch our hearts.
Though such inventions may just flop,
We'll laugh and dream, we'll never stop.

With chocolate rivers, orange skies,
In this wild world, we'll fantasize.
Every oddity's worth a try,
As laughter echoes in the sky.

Echoes of the Unfathomed

In the forest filled with bees,
I chase my thoughts on summer's breeze.
They buzz and swirl, they dance around,
In chaos, joy is truly found.

Climbing trees to reach the stars,
I find a moonbeam in my jars.
A squirrel waves, then rolls his eyes,
At all my wild, unplanned surprise.

The rivers sing a silly tune,
As I splash 'neath the cheeky moon.
With every turn and twist of fate,
I giggle loud, I celebrate.

Who knew adventure turned out fun,
Like ice cream melting in the sun?
With every echo, laughter sings,
Life's playful, full of little things.

The Symphony of Choices

A melody of forks and spoons,
Plays out beneath the lopsided moons.
I choose to wear my socks, mismatched,
While serenading what I've hatched.

The music swells as cookies bake,
And every rhythm's up for take.
With vegetables in pirate hats,
I twirl and laugh with all the spats.

When life's a song of silly tunes,
You find the fun in afternoon.
So grab a broomstick, let's all jive,
In quirky battles, we'll survive.

Each note a flavor, wild and free,
A dish of choices, who's with me?
In this grand symphony we make,
We gather joy in every break.

Bubbles of Inspiration in a Chaotic Sea

In a world so wild and bright,
I chased a bubble in flight,
It danced and swayed, full of cheer,
Then popped, and I yelled, 'Oh dear!'

With laughter echoing all around,
I found my footing on shaky ground,
Each stumble turned into a laugh,
Who knew chaos could be such a craft?

Sprinkling joy like confetti confounded,
In waves of fun, we all grounded,
We built a fortress of giggles and glee,
On this hilarious and chaotic sea.

So let the bubbles float high,
While we slip and slide, oh my!
In a whirl of bubbles and merry play,
Who needs calm on this wild day?

Wings of the Unseen

Invisible wings flap above,
They carry us, not push or shove,
Like errant kites, we twist and turn,
In silly spirals, we yearn and learn.

With each gust, we take to flight,
A belly flop is pure delight,
We soar, we crash, we laugh anew,
In the dance of risks, I cling to you.

Our shadows flit on the sunny ground,
Like whispers of mischief, they astound,
So we leap like jelly beans in the air,
With wings of laughs, we have no care.

Embrace the silliness we weave,
As unseen wings help us believe,
In the joy of absurdity's embrace,
Flying high in this goofy space.

Radiance in the Mist

Fog rolls in, a curtain of gray,
But I'm here, ready to play,
Like a glow worm in a sock drawer,
I shine bright, but who knows what for?

With misplaced joy, I trip and tumble,
Creating laughter with each fumble,
In a world so murky, I find a light,
Sparking giggles, as I take flight.

Misty mornings bring a foggy delight,
As we chase the sparkle hidden from sight,
With raincoats on, and hearts so bold,
We weave through the haze, stories unfold.

So let's dance in this world unclear,
Finding brightness is quite sincere,
Through the mist, our spirits will lift,
In a play of joy, we find our gift.

A Tapestry of Longing

Woven dreams in a blanket of cheer,
I stitch my wishes, year after year,
Each thread a giggle, a hope, a jest,
A cozy quilt that feels like a fest.

In patterns of chaos, I sew my fun,
With patches of sunshine and laughter spun,
Dancing along with a needle and thread,
In the fabric of life, no tear goes unsaid.

Colorful wishes tangled in time,
A tapestry bright, where my thoughts rhyme,
So I weave through the fabric, my heart on display,
In the loom of existence, I'll play and sway.

Pull on my heartstrings, let laughter resound,
In this happy quilt, joy is profound,
For longing can spark the silliest dreams,
As I craft my vision with playful themes.

Echoes in the Void of Possibility

In a world where socks go solo,
And left shoes dance with pride,
I ponder deep in my taco,
Wondering if it's all a ride.

With gravity on holiday,
I float on mashed potato dreams,
Finding wisdom in the delay,
While my cat plots schemes to bite my seams.

Life's like playing charades with time,
Striking poses, haphazardly fine,
I ask for signs, read the mime,
Is pizza the meaning of the divine?

So here I am, still on this track,
With googly eyes and a rubber chicken,
Embracing chaos, never look back,
It's the thrill of finding the missing chicken!

Brushstrokes of Imperfection

I once painted a masterpiece,
With a brush dipped in spaghetti sauce,
Can't tell if it's art or a lease,
But I swear it's got some sauce.

My canvas is a cereal box,
Each crunch a note in my tune,
Jackpots of joy in stickered socks,
While I sip my milk on a moon.

The colors clash, the lines may blur,
But art's not perfect, that's the game,
My neighbor thinks it's a bit of a stir,
I just call it my claim to fame.

Embracing whoopee cushions in style,
I laugh at rules, dismiss perfection,
For life's a canvas, bright and vile,
And I'd rather paint a fun connection!

A Journey Through the Lingering Unknown

I wandered down a candy lane,
Unraveled by an odd sensation,
Thought I found the meaning of gain,
But tripped on my own imagination.

A map made out of confetti dots,
Leading straight to a chocolate stream,
I pondered life, forgot my thoughts,
And woke up in a gummy dream.

Questions squirm like jelly worms,
While my shoes giggle at my plight,
Is it wisdom or just quirky terms?
I laugh and keep chasing the light.

Onward through this silly quest,
With a twinkling eye and a funny bone,
I dance like a marshmallow in jest,
Singing tunes that are quite my own!

Embracing the Wilderness Within

Deep in the jungle of my mind,
I find lost treasure: a fork and knife,
In between thoughts of every kind,
Anticipating the dinner of life.

Squirrels in bow ties take a stroll,
Debating whether to climb or hide,
While my heart beats like a drumroll,
Each twitch, a laugh from inside.

The wild side calls with a rubber band,
Releasing giggles, a hoot, a snicker,
Every moment feels unplanned,
In this chaos, I become quicker.

So I embrace this wild parade,
With mismatched shoes and a sun-kissed grin,
For in this untamed escapade,
I'm living free and don't need to win!

Tethered to Tomorrow

In a world where socks just disappear,
I ponder where they go, oh dear!
Hopping on one foot, a clumsy dance,
Life's little quirks, a wild romance.

With coffee spills and laughter loud,
I trip on dreams, a jesting crowd.
Chasing rainbows in my backyard,
Life's a circus, but oh, not hard!

Each sunset paints a silly frown,
Yet mornings greet me with a crown.
Tethered to moments full of jest,
In this grand chaos, I feel blessed.

So here I stand, with mismatched shoes,
Waving my flag of joyful blues.
Tomorrow beckons, yet I'm still here,
Singing my song, a heart sincere.

Vignettes of Unspoken Hope

Beneath a veil of melting cheese,
I eat my way through life with ease.
Sundaes tall with cherry tops,
Unspoken wishes never stop.

In line for dreams, a goofy wait,
I ponder all that might be fate.
A hula hoop, I spin with glee,
Life's a surprise, just wait and see!

With wild ideas like tossing pies,
I navigate the world with sighs.
Each giggle echoes, sweet and free,
A portrait of what's yet to be.

Still, I stroll through fields of sun,
Wearing a smile, just having fun.
Hope's a kite stuck in a tree,
But I'll get it down, just wait for me!

An Odyssey of Unfulfilled Wishes

Once I wished for a pet giraffe,
But ended up with a grumpy calf.
Still, I feed it dreams and hay,
In my cozy corner, we'll play all day.

A spaceship made of paper dreams,
Took me on journeys bursting at seams.
Yet I found myself back in bed,
With cosmic crumbs left in my head.

My coffee's strong, but so is the laugh,
A backdrop for my silly staff.
With friends like these, the wishes wane,
But they fill my heart, like sunshine rain.

An odyssey carved in moments bright,
Filled with blunders that feel just right.
We'll dance through wishes, boisterous and bold,
For in each laughter, life's stories unfold.

The Unfolding Tapestry of Days

Threaded patterns of joy and cheer,
Weaves a tapestry of days sincere.
Laughter stitches the fraying seams,
In a world spun of whimsical dreams.

From breakfast flops on Sunday morn,
To buzzing bees where flowers are born.
Each moment colors a joyous thread,
A patchwork quilt where we all tread.

So let's twirl in mismatched socks,
And doodle writings on our clocks.
For every giggle and hearty cheer,
Unfolds the magic, bringing us near.

In this brave scheme of clock and spoon,
We twirl like leaves under the moon.
Each day's a dance, come join the fray,
In the lively puzzle of our play.

When Paths Converge

Two roads met in a wacky dance,
One wore shoes, the other, pants.
They laughed and joked, a funny scene,
As they debated where they'd been.

A squirrel watched with questioning eyes,
Taking notes on their strange replies.
What if the shoes gave it a fright?
And the pants just fled into the night?

The paths all twisted in a playful spin,
No one could tell where it would begin.
They spun in circles, cheeks puffed out,
Creating chaos without a doubt.

By the end, they both were sore,
But couldn't help but want to explore.
With giggles echoing through the trees,
They set off, determined to find some cheese.

Embracing the Unwritten Tomorrow

What's going on tomorrow? Who can say?
A llama may lead us to play!
Or a toast with jam and silly hats,
A dance-off with cranky old cats.

I filled my jar with dreams last night,
Capricious wishes, oh what a sight!
Juggling future and past with flair,
While my cat gives me a judging stare.

The weather's forecast is purely absurd,
Rainbow sprinkles and cotton candy birds.
Grapes might rain and time may freeze,
In a world where we just do as we please.

With maps all drawn in crayon hues,
We'll stumble through mistakes, and chase good views.
So raise a toast to tomorrows unsung,
Where laughter blooms and we stay young!

Labyrinths of Living

In a maze of dreams, I had a snack,
Mice played chess, I joined the pack.
We wandered round in circles tight,
Or was it just a funny sight?

Ducks broke out in a tap dance spree,
While I tried to solve the mystery.
Who let the goats in this enchanted place?
They wore little hats, each with their grace.

I took a step, but what's this fright?
A hedgehog yelled, "Stay out all night!"
We laughed so hard the walls did shake,
In a labyrinth of joy, we'd never break.

Just me and my pals, and twisting ways,
Chasing rainbows through funny days.
If life's a maze, let's lose our way,
And make some memories here today!

Tides of Time Unfolding

The clock ticks funny, like a clown,
Wearing big shoes and a bright red frown.
Minutes chase seconds, what a race!
Tickle fights with time, just for grace.

The waves come in with giggly glee,
Fish wearing hats swim close to me.
A whale yodels in a silly tune,
While stars come out to dance with the moon.

Shall we ride on time's own tide?
With rubber ducks, let's take a slide!
Each bubble popped is a laugh on shore,
Waves tickle toes; who could want more?

So here we sail, on laughter's stream,
With a wink and a smirk, we'll chase our dream.
In this wave of time, we'll take our stand,
Holding hands and hearts, forever grand.

Glimmers of Growth in Shadowed Places

In gardens of doubt, flowers bloom bright,
They giggle at ghosts that dance in the night.
With sunshine and rain, they're never alone,
Even weeds toss a party, they've all overgrown.

The shadows can't stop a wildflower's cheer,
As daisies debate if they're brave or sincere.
A snail on a mission moves slow but with glee,
In the dirt lies a secret, just waiting for me.

Amongst all the chaos, there's joy in the mess,
Like socks in a dryer, we find our success.
With roots intertwined, they laugh at the fight,
Embracing the weird; they shine through the night.

So let's tiptoe lightly on paths they have crossed,
In gardens of whimsy, let's never feel lost.
For with every stumble, new magic we'll see,
In glimmers of hope, we just need to be free.

Meandering Through the Maze of Many

In a labyrinth crafted of each silly choice,
We chase after laughter, we dance and rejoice.
With each twist and turn, a new joke pops up,
Like running through circles with a clown in a cup.

A hedgehog confesses his love for a hat,
While squirrels spill secrets that fall from their chat.
Gazing at rabbit holes luring us down,
We giggle at life as it tilts us around.

Through corridors crowded with quaint, quirky sights,
We navigate friendships and hilarious nights.
A mix-up of socks, and a sock puppet show,
In the maze of the many, let silliness flow.

So hold on to fun as we wander the path,
In this maze of delight, find the joy like a bath.
For while we are lost, it's the laughter we find,
That colors our journey and eases the mind.

A Song for the Unraveled

Oh turn up the tunes for the tangled and torn,
Like yarn that's unwound on a bright autumn morn.
With melodies mixed, and some notes out of key,
This symphony's chaos is perfect for me.

The drums play a rhythm of socks taking flight,
As coffee spills caffeine on the paper so white.
With giggles and grumbles, we twirl and we spin,
In the unspooling tale, let the journey begin.

We dance with the odd ones, the quirks in our song,
Like moths to the flame, we all sing along.
As verses unravel, our laughter will soar,
Creating a chorus that echoes for more.

So grab your old rhythms, and let them run free,
In the riddle of life, find the joy to agree.
With each note and pause, we'll make it a spree,
A song for the unwrapped, come sing out with me!

Threads of Memories Yet to Be Woven

In the loom of our past, where the stories all blend,
We gather the moments, like gifts from a friend.
With needles of laughter and thread made of dreams,
We weave through the chaos, or so it seems.

The fabric of time has its patches and tears,
With elephants dancing and odd rubber bears.
Through colors that clash and the patterns that fray,
We find all the joy in the fibers of play.

Each thread pulls us closer, entwined like a hug,
While memories tangle, they fit like a snug.
We unravel the gloom with a smile and a grin,
Intertwined like the laughter, where does it begin?

So stitch with abandon, let creativity flow,
In the quilt of existence, there's room for the glow.
For the threads still unspooled carry hopes yet to see,
In the tapestry living, come stitch along with me.

Navigating Through Fog and Light

In a world painted gray, I drift and I sway,
Like a sailor lost, looking for the day.
With my map upside down, I laugh at my plight,
Stumbling through shadows, chasing the light.

Oh, the things that I see, in this foggy disguise,
A jellyfish waltzing, beneath cloudy skies.
My compass spins wildly, spins a tale quite absurd,
I chase after whispers, while talking to birds.

With the sky overhead, a patchwork of cheer,
I trip on a thought, but I've no time for fear.
For I dance with the winds, and I shout with delight,
Who needs a clear path, when it's fun to invite?

So here's to my journey, with laughter in tow,
In the land of the lost, watch my confusion grow!
I'll navigate life, with my eyes full of glee,
For every misstep, unlocks more to see.

Footprints on the Road Less Taken

With a shoe full of mud, I march where I please,
Following footprints that lead to my knees.
With a grin on my face, I stumble with flair,
Hopscotch with raccoons, in a daft little square.

Oh, the folks must be wondering, what's wrong with my tread,
Why I'm waltzing through puddles instead of my bed?
But each splash is a joy, a giggle, a cheer,
As I dance with my shadow, who's never sincere.

The road less taken's filled with sweet pranks,
A parade of mishaps, potential hijinks.
With breadcrumbs of laughter, I leave on my way,
For every lost grain leads to another buffet.

So here's to the chaos, the fun twists and turns,
To the bright, silly antics, and the lessons life earns.
In the footprints I leave, may the echoes proclaim,
That the joy of the journey is the heart of the game.

Labyrinths of Endless Possibility

In a maze made of giggles, I wander around,
Every turn that I take leads to new joys abound.
With walls made of candy and ceilings of glee,
I skip through this labyrinth, feeling quite free.

Oh, where do I go? Left, right, or straight?
A clown holds a sign that says, 'Choose your own fate!'
With a wink and a nod, he juggles my thoughts,
And suddenly I'm pondering giant tea pots.

Every twist and each corner shows wonders galore,
A parade of lost socks, and a few cats that snore.
I trip over rabbit holes, laughter takes flight,
In the labyrinth's depths, my worries feel light.

I'll give myself time, to bask in the maze,
With every wrong turn, I find new pathways.
For in this big puzzle of colors and cheer,
I've learned that the journey is truly the sphere.

Currents of Change in Still Waters

In waters so still, the ripples make laughter,
With a fish in a tie, swimming on after.
He quips, 'Don't you know, change is a dance?
Just wiggle your fins and give chance a chance!'

With a splash and a giggle, I dive right on in,
Turning stillness to motion, oh, let the fun begin!
For in every slow swirl, a whirlwind will wake,
And a rubber duck joins as the currents I make.

The calm hides a chorus, of quirks yet to find,
While turtles play chess, so patient, so kind.
With each paddle stroke, a new twist reveals,
In the calm of stillness, adventure appeals.

So, let's ride these waves of whimsy and play,
With a splash and a giggle, we'll brighten the gray.
For change is the magic in life's gentle stream,
And I'm here for the laughter, the fun, and the dream.

Chronicles of Unfinished Journeys

In purple socks and mismatched shoes,
We wander paths we didn't choose.
Each map we draw, a wild delight,
Yet always lost before it's night.

We sketch the clouds with silly pens,
Debate which burger tops the trends.
With fridge magnets as our guide,
We steer through chaos, joy, and pride.

The suitcase squeaks, it's filled with dreams,
Yet half of it just bursts at seams.
With laughter echoing wide and clear,
We toast to roads and half our beer.

The journey's pace is full of jest,
As we lose track of every quest.
With ice cream drips and laughter loud,
Adventure calls — we're feeling proud.

Whispers of the Unyielding Heart

We chase our whims with open arms,
Defying rules, embracing charms.
Life's like a buffet, taste it all,
From pickle pop to toffee fall.

Our hearts, they race, yet trip and slip,
On banana peels, with silly quips.
The dance of fate, a wobbly spin,
In every loss, we find to win.

We carve our paths through quest and fun,
Like kids who never see the sun.
With glee we shout, "Let's try that next!"
While fate rolls dice, we're feeling vexed.

Still, laughter blooms in every space,
And silly grins light up each face.
What's next, dear heart? A plate of fries?
Life sings sweet tunes, in mad disguise.

A Canvas of Unwritten Stories

With brushes dipped in rainbow hues,
We paint the day, ignore the blues.
Our canvas waits for bold strokes bright,
As ideas swirl in giggles light.

The sun's a brush, the moon a pen,
Creating tales again and again.
Each splash of paint, a burst of cheer,
A little chaos, a little fear.

In every corner, whispers tease,
Like cotton candy in the breeze.
We write instead of bite the dust,
In rubber boots, we kick up rust.

So hand in hand, we paint the night,
With splattered hopes and hearts in flight.
Each untold tale, a giggle's tune,
We dance beneath the watchful moon.

Echoes of Tomorrow's Dreams

Tomorrow calls, a jester's grin,
With plans that make us chuckle thin.
We toss our dreams in backpacks high,
Yet trip on shoelaces, oh my my!

With every sketch, a future bright,
Yet naps compete with starry night.
The clock ticks loud, yet we just grin,
As last week's laundry fills with sin.

In every echo, laughter rings,
While flying pigs sprout silly wings.
We take to skies with silly hats,
And share our snacks with friendly cats.

Though plans may twist, and chaos reign,
Our spirits soar, we feel no pain.
With dreams that dance in wobbly airs,
We catch the joy, and share our cares.

Starlit Reflections on a New Path

Under twinkling skies, I take a step,
Fumbling like a cat, but no room for prep.
Moonbeams chuckle as I trip and twirl,
Is this the way or just the night's whirl?

Each star, a wink, saying, 'Keep your cheer!'
I dance with shadows, banishing fear.
Every tumble's a badge, a tale to spin,
"Look at me," I laugh, "I'm trying to win!"

A path of giggles, I forge along,
Serenading squirrels with my own song.
They pause, they nod, as if they can see,
That life is best when you're just being free.

So here's to the blunders, the trips we take,
With starlit reflections on a night so fake.
One step ahead, and oh, look at the view,
Life's delight is found in the silly, so true!

Patterns of Resilience and Renewal

Patterns emerge like clouds in the sky,
Some float on by, while others comply.
Life's tapestry weaves with plenty of flair,
Every twist and turn, a new tale to share.

Resilience winks, saying, 'Not so fast!'
I trip on my goals, but I'm having a blast.
Renewal whispers, 'Try it once more!'
Watch me juggle dreams 'til I drop on the floor.

Through giggles and guffaws, I wade through the mess,
Making friends with my failings, I seldom feel stress.
Each pattern a lesson, each bump a new chance,
In this crazy dance, at least I can prance.

So let's laugh at the chaos, embrace the charm,
With resilience as armor, we'll weather the storm.
In patterns so quirky, we find our own strength,
With humor as guide, we'll go the great length.

Cascades of Serendipity

Oh, cascades of laughter, tumbling along,
Life's silly surprises are my favorite song.
From mishaps and blunders, rich gems are found,
Like tripping on shoelaces, I bounce off the ground.

Serendipity dances in colors so bright,
With a wink and a nudge, say, 'What's left or right?'
I wander these paths like a lost little pup,
But every detour is a pick-me-up!

A banana peel's lurking, a slip and a fall,
In these moments, I'm having a ball.
Who knew happiness lived in such bliss?
My journey's a giggle, I'd never want this!

So here's to the not-so-serious ride,
With cascades of wonder, let laughter be our guide.
For every twist and tumble, we'll seize with delight,
Let's celebrate moments that sparkle so bright!

Unturned Stones of Potential

In a field of choices, I flip every stone,
What's hiding beneath? A treasure unknown.
With giggles that echo, I dare to explore,
Each bump in the road, a secret to store.

Unturned and uncertain, potential abounds,
Like a puppy chasing wildly through the grounds.
I gather my dreams like daisies in bloom,
While side-stepping calamities, avoiding the gloom.

Beneath every rock lies a story to tell,
From grins to the groans, I embrace them all well.
With laughter my lantern, I wander the way,
Finding joy in the mishaps that brighten my day.

So here's to the journeys, all quirky and strange,
As I dance through the rocks, I'll never feel range.
For each unturned stone holds wonders galore,
In the mess of potential, I'm always wanting more!

www.ingramcontent.com/pod-product-compliance
Lightning Source LLC
Chambersburg PA
CBHW051640160426
43209CB00004B/731